EB LINCOLN   3483998

Abraham

Mount Rushmore Presidential Series

Frank Keating
&
Mike Wimmer

A Paula Wiseman Book
Simon & Schuster Books for Young Readers
New York London Toronto Sydney New Delhi

IN THIS TEMPLE
AS IN THE HEARTS OF THE PEOPLE
FOR WHOM HE SAVED THE UNION
THE MEMORY OF ABRAHAM LINCOLN
IS ENSHRINED FOREVER

*F*ather Abraham.

Honest Abe.

The Great Emancipator.

I was also the sixteenth president of the United
States of America.

I liberated the slaves.

I saved the Union.

Early on, though, I wasn't expected to amount to much.

"It is a great piece of folly to attempt to make anything out of my early life."

It really can be summarized by a single phrase. My childhood was a part of the "short and simple annals of the poor."

There was little that could be said about me because "there (was) not much of me."

I was born on February 12, 1809, in a Kentucky cabin with a packed-dirt floor, rough slab roof, and a leather-hinged door, all held in place by poles and stones.

It had one room and a single window.

My clothes were sewn from cloth spun by my mother or fashioned from the skin of animals shot by my father. I helped with the chores. I carried water from the creek. I hoed weeds, picked berries, and grubbed for walnuts, hickory, and hazelnuts.

Our suppers were simple and mostly wild game: turkey, partridge, rabbit, deer, and bear.

I walked barefoot for most of the year, through all the seasons.

I saw myself as "humble Abraham Lincoln" because "I was born and have ever remained in the most humble walks of life."

I went to school "by littles." All together, it did not amount to one year. Our books were few but important: the Bible, Webster's *Spelling Book*, and *Pike's Arithmetic*.

Books opened my eyes. They captured my mind.

Reading was everything to me.

As I grew tall and strong, I worked hard. I cleared timber for pastures for livestock and corn. I burned brush, split rails, milked cows, churned butter, and cured hides of raccoon and deer.

Heavy toil.

Hard work is the most persistent memory of my youth.

My free time was consumed by books. Any books. All books. Through thicket and thorn I scoured for books. I once walked twenty miles to borrow a book.

"The things I want to know are in books."

I also read and wrote poetry and rhyme. My pen was a turkey buzzard feather tipped with ink from a blackberry briar root. Sometimes I wrote silly verses: "Abraham Lincoln, his hand and pen, he will be good but God knows when."

From Kentucky to Indiana and eventually to Illinois. As my family moved, my circle remained those that I loved. And my books. I read and memorized what I could. If I had no paper to write on, I used wooden boards.

I loved to be with people. I occasionally jumped onto a tree stump or stood on a fence to talk to my fellow workers. My father frequently made me stop to return to work.

I often traveled across the Ohio River and down the Mississippi—running a ferryboat or a flatboat for goods. I continued to learn. I listened to speeches; I heard legal arguments in court. I was alert to new ideas. I absorbed it all: by sight, by scent, by sound.

In Illinois, I worked as a store clerk. I read late and arose early to read. I always carried a book under my arm. When I was the postmaster of New Salem, I carried the mail in my hat. I also worked as a surveyor, a storekeeper, a mill hand, a soldier, and a legislator.

I continued to read. And to study. And to debate the issues of the day. I became a lawyer without legal training, which was often remarked upon as the envy of many.

I moved to Springfield and studied the law, seated at a rough wooden table, warmed by an old woodstove and a buffalo hide.

The law was my love. I resolved to be a peacemaker. I vowed to make good morals a part of my law practice. I determined "to be honest at all events." I believed that if one cannot be an honest lawyer, he should at least "resolve to be honest without being a lawyer."

I knew that hard work was my only path. Truthfulness and fair dealing in law and in business resulted in my being called Honest Abe.

I prospered as a lawyer and met Mary, married, and became a father. My neighbors continued to trust and respect me. They elected me to a brief term in Congress.

My ambition was simple and straightforward: to be "truly esteemed of my fellow man."

But the times were unsettled. Passion and controversy roiled the land.

Everywhere, people began to ask whether it was right that one man could own another. Some said that ownership of one by another was protected by the Constitution. Others argued that the Union promised a new life for ordinary people, free and limited only by the imagination and ambition of its citizens.

I believed that the Declaration of Independence was a "charter of freedom" for all people, black and white.

"He who would be no slave, must consent to have no slave. Those who deny freedom to others, deserve it not for themselves. . . ."

"If slavery is not wrong, nothing is wrong."

I was determined to secure freedom for others and to assure the union of our states.

Freedom and union had pulled me up from a "hired" laborer, little better than a slave, to a "society of equals." I could not stand by and see it end.

I knew that "there can be no moral right with one man making a slave of another."

Though not in office, I would not remain silent. The country was ablaze with emotion and conflict. It appeared that disunion and slavery would shatter our splintering land.

I stood for one people and one land. I traveled the country. I entered the fray. My voice was heard. People listened. I was elected the sixteenth president of the United States. People were convinced a "house divided" cannot stand. Our wonderful land could not remain half slave and half free.

Though I hoped the "better angels of our nature" would hold us together, I was wrong. The country broke apart.

Blue versus gray. North versus South. Brother versus brother. War and bloodshed. The agony appeared endless.

Defeat. Darkness. Destruction. And from some, despair.

"We cannot escape history. . . . The fiery trial through which we pass, will light us down, in honor or dishonor, to the latest generation."

But I always knew that this nation, under God, would survive. We were "the last, best hope of earth." America must survive. America must prevail.

My goal never changed. My resolve never faltered.

Union and freedom. Forever.

"With malice toward none, with charity for all," the nation would become one again.

The sparkling call for equality and dignity for each person emblazoned in the Declaration of Independence would be embraced by all and enjoyed by all, now and tomorrow.

This conflict was a "people's contest," to "elevate the condition of men . . ."—all men—"to afford all an unfettered start and a fair chance, in the race of life."

The Civil War was finally won. The experiment was nobly saved.

The Union survived.

Every man was free.

Man's best hopes of equal opportunity and equal rights would not perish from the earth.

Address Delivered at the Dedication
of the Cemetery at Gettysburg

Abraham Lincoln

NOVEMBER 19, 1863

Four score and seven years ago our fathers brought forth on this continent, a new nation, conceived in Liberty, and dedicated to the proposition that all men are created equal.

Now we are engaged in a great civil war, testing whether that nation, or any nation so conceived and dedicated, can long endure. We are met on a great battlefield of that war. We have come to dedicate a portion of that field, as a final resting place for those who here gave their lives that that nation might live. It is altogether fitting and proper that we should do this.

But, in a larger sense, we cannot dedicate—we cannot consecrate—we cannot hallow—this ground. The brave men, living and dead, who struggled here, have consecrated it, far above our poor power to add or detract. The world will little note, nor long remember what we say here, but it can never forget what they did here. It is for us the living, rather, to be dedicated here to the unfinished work which they who fought here have thus far so nobly advanced. It is rather for us to be here dedicated to the great task remaining before us—that from these honored dead we take increased devotion to that cause for which they gave the last full measure of devotion—that we here highly resolve that these dead shall not have died in vain—that this nation, under God, shall have a new birth of freedom—and that government of the people, by the people, for the people, shall not perish from the earth.

The life of Abraham Lincoln was an affirmation of the unprecedented call of the Declaration of Independence that all men are created equal. Unheard of when written and marked by reverses and resistance since its utterance, it remains the fundamental law of the land. This book is dedicated to those who have stood for equality since Lincoln's day. To those who have lived with firmness and resolve that race, color, sex, and nationality can play no role in halting the progress of all to be one.
—F. K.

To my three sons, Eli, Holden, and Broden, who have all helped to bring Abraham alive by modeling for me. I hope that he will also be a model for you.
—M. W.

ACKNOWLEDGMENTS

The illustrator gratefully acknowledges Dan Storck, supervisor of Mount Vernon, who modeled as President Lincoln, and Hilary Malson, marketing and membership coordinator for President Lincoln's Cottage, a Site of the National Trust for Historic Preservation, for their help in researching and creating this book.

BIBLIOGRAPHY

There are many great books on Abraham Lincoln. This is a list of those I referred to while writing this book.—F. K.

Beveridge, Albert J. *Abraham Lincoln 1809–1858*. Vol. 1. Boston: Houghton Mifflin, 1928.

Gallagher, Gary W. *The Union War*. Cambridge, MA: Harvard University Press, 2011.

Guelzo, Allen C. "Our Lincoln." *National Review*. February 23, 2009.

Lincoln, Abraham. *Lincoln: Speeches and Writings 1832–1858*. Edited by Don E. Fehrenbacher. New York: Library of America, 1989.

McPherson, James M. *Abraham Lincoln and the Second American Revolution*. London: Oxford University Press, 1991.

Nicolay, John G. *A Short Life of Abraham Lincoln*. New York: The Century Company, 1903.

Pratt, Harry E. *Concerning Mr. Lincoln*. Springfield, IL: Abraham Lincoln Association, 1944.

Sandburg, Carl. *Abraham Lincoln: The Prairie Years*. New York: Harcourt Brace, 1926.

Simon, Paul. *Lincoln's Preparation for Greatness*. Norman, OK: OU Press, 1965.

Thomas, Benjamin P. *Abraham Lincoln: A Biography*. New York: Modern Library, 1968.

Wilson, Douglas L. *Honor's Voice: The Transformation of Abraham Lincoln*. New York: Knopf, 1999.

All quotations are the words of Abraham Lincoln.

SIMON & SCHUSTER BOOKS FOR YOUNG READERS

An imprint of Simon & Schuster Children's Publishing Division • 1230 Avenue of the Americas, New York, New York 10020

Text copyright © 2017 by Frank Keating • Illustrations copyright © 2017 by Mike Wimmer

SIMON & SCHUSTER BOOKS FOR YOUNG READERS is a trademark of Simon & Schuster, Inc.

For information about special discounts for bulk purchases, please contact Simon & Schuster Special Sales at 1-866-506-1949 or business@simonandschuster.com

The Simon & Schuster Speakers Bureau can bring authors to your live event. For more information or to book an event, contact the Simon & Schuster Speakers Bureau at 1-866-248-3049 or visit our website at www.simonspeakers.com.

Book design by Chloë Foglia • The text for this book was set in Old Claude. • The illustrations for this book were rendered in oil on canvas.

Manufactured in China • 1016 SCP • First Edition

2 4 6 8 10 9 7 5 3 1

Library of Congress Cataloging-in-Publication Data

Names: Keating, Francis Anthony, 1944– | Wimmer, Mike, illustrator.

Title: Abraham / Frank Keating ; illustrated by Mike Wimmer.

Description: 1st edition. | New York : Simon & Schuster Books for Young Readers, 2017. | Series: A Paula Wiseman book

Identifiers: LCCN 2013015823| ISBN 9781442493193 (hardcover) | ISBN 9781442493209 (eBook)

Subjects: LCSH: Lincoln, Abraham, 1809–1865—Juvenile literature. | Presidents—United States—Biography—Juvenile literature.

Classification: LCC E457.905 .K43 2017 | DDC 973.7092—dc23 LC record available at http://lccn.loc.gov/2013015823